SIPS & SNACKS

Publications International, Ltd.

Louis Weber, CEO
Publications International, Ltd.
8140 Lehigh Ave
Morton Grove, IL 60053

Pictured on the front cover: Bloody Mary *(page 12).*

Pictured on the back cover *(clockwise from top left):* Martinez *(page 5),* Parmesan Garlic Monkey Bread *(page 92),* White Spinach Queso *(page 164),* Aviation *(page 36)* and Churros *(page 156).*

ISBN: 978-1-63938-833-2

Manufactured in China.

8 7 6 5 4 3 2 1

Microwave Cooking: Microwave ovens vary in wattage. Use the cooking times as guidelines and check for doneness before adding more time.

WARNING: Food preparation, baking and cooking involve inherent dangers: misuse of electric products, sharp electric tools, boiling water, hot stoves, allergic reactions, foodborne illnesses and the like, pose numerous potential risks. Publications International, Ltd. (PIL) assumes no responsibility or liability for any damages you may experience as a result of following recipes, instructions, tips or advice in this publication.

While we hope this publication helps you find new ways to eat delicious foods, you may not always achieve the results desired due to variations in ingredients, cooking temperatures, typos, errors, omissions or individual cooking abilities.

According to the Surgeon General, women should not drink alcoholic beverages during pregnancy because of the risk of birth defects. Consumption of alcoholic beverages impairs your ability to drive a car or operate machinery and may cause health problems. If you drink, do not drive.

Let's get social!

@Publications_International

@PublicationsInternational

www.pilbooks.com

CONTENTS

CLASSIC COCKTAILS

MARTINEZ

MAKES 1 SERVING

- 1½ ounces gin
- ¾ ounce sweet vermouth
- ½ ounce maraschino liqueur
- 2 dashes orange bitters
- Lemon or orange twist

Fill cocktail shaker half full with ice; add gin, vermouth, liqueur and bitters. Shake about 20 seconds or until very cold; strain into coupe or cocktail glass. Garnish with lemon twist.

NEW YORK SOUR

MAKES 1 SERVING

- 2 ounces rye or bourbon whiskey
- 1 ounce lemon juice
- ¾ ounce simple syrup (page 6)
- 1 ounce dry red wine

Fill cocktail shaker half full with ice; add whiskey, lemon juice and simple syrup. Shake until blended and very cold. Strain into old-fashioned glass. Carefully pour wine over back of spoon just above surface of cocktail; do not stir.

SOUTH SIDE >

MAKES 1 SERVING

- 2 ounces gin
- ¾ ounce lemon juice
- ¾ ounce simple syrup (recipe follows)
- 5 fresh mint leaves
- Fresh mint sprig and lemon twist

Fill cocktail shaker half full with ice; add gin, lemon juice, simple syrup and mint leaves. Shake until blended; strain into ice-filled Collins glass or cocktail glass. Garnish with mint sprig and lemon twist.

SIMPLE SYRUP

Combine 1 cup water and 1 cup sugar in small saucepan. Cook over medium heat just until sugar is dissolved, stirring frequently. Cool to room temperature; store syrup in glass jar in refrigerator.

BOULEVARDIER

MAKES 1 SERVING

- 1½ ounces bourbon whiskey
- 1 ounce sweet vermouth
- 1 ounce Campari
- Orange slice or twist

Fill mixing glass or cocktail shaker half full with ice; add bourbon, vermouth and Campari. Stir 30 seconds or until cold; strain into old fashioned or cocktail glass. Garnish with orange slice.

FRENCH MARTINI >

MAKES 1 SERVING

- 2 ounces vodka
- 2 ounces pineapple juice
- ½ ounce raspberry liqueur

Fill cocktail shaker half full with ice; add vodka, pineapple juice and liqueur. Shake until blended; strain into cocktail glass.

GRASSHOPPER

MAKES 1 SERVING

- 2 ounces crème de menthe
- 2 ounces crème de cacao
- 2 ounces half-and-half or whipping cream

Fill cocktail shaker half full with ice; add liqueurs and half-and-half. Shake until blended; strain into cocktail glass.

TUXEDO COCKTAIL

MAKES 1 SERVING

- 1½ ounces gin
- 1 ounce dry vermouth
- ½ teaspoon maraschino liqueur
- ¼ teaspoon absinthe or Pernod
- 2 dashes orange bitters
- Maraschino cherry

Fill mixing glass or cocktail shaker half full with ice; add gin, vermouth, liqueur, absinthe and bitters. Stir 30 seconds or until very cold; strain into cocktail glass. Garnish with maraschino cherry.

MOJITO >

MAKES 2 SERVINGS

- 8 fresh mint leaves, plus additional sprigs for garnish
- 2 ounces lime juice
- 2 teaspoons superfine sugar or powdered sugar
- 3 ounces light rum
- Chilled club soda or seltzer
- 2 lime slices

Combine half of mint leaves, lime juice and sugar in each of two highball glasses; mash with wooden spoon or muddler. Fill glasses with ice. Pour rum over ice; top with club soda. Garnish with lime slices and additional mint leaves.

MANHATTAN

MAKES 1 SERVING

- 2 ounces whiskey
- 1 ounce sweet vermouth
- 1 dash Angostura bitters
- Maraschino cherry

Fill cocktail shaker half full with ice; add whiskey, vermouth and bitters. Stir 30 seconds or until very cold until blended; strain into chilled cocktail glass or ice-filled old fashioned glass. Garnish with maraschino cherry.

BLOODY MARY >

MAKES 1 SERVING

- 1 dash *each* Worcestershire sauce, hot pepper sauce, celery salt, black pepper and salt
- 3 ounces tomato juice
- 1½ ounces vodka
- ½ ounce lemon juice
- Lime slice, celery stalk with leaves, pickle spear and/or green olives

Fill highball glass with ice; add dashes of Worcestershire sauce, hot pepper sauce, celery salt, black pepper and salt. Add tomato juice, vodka and lemon juice; stir until blended. Serve with desired garnishes.

CAESAR

Substitute clam tomato juice for the tomato juice.

VICEROY

MAKES 1 SERVING

- 1½ ounces pisco
- 1 ounce Lillet Blanc
- ½ ounce lime juice
- ½ ounce simple syrup (page 6)
- 1½ ounces chilled tonic water
- Fresh mint sprig

Combine pisco, Lillet Blanc, lime juice and simple syrup in ice-filled highball glass. Top with tonic water; stir until blended. Garnish with mint.

SIDECAR >

MAKES 1 SERVING

- 2 ounces brandy or cognac
- 2 ounces triple sec
- ½ ounce lemon juice
- Orange twist

Fill cocktail shaker half full with ice; add brandy, triple sec and lemon juice. Shake until blended; strain into cocktail glass. Garnish with orange twist.

WHISKEY SMASH

MAKES 1 SERVING

- 2 lemon quarters
- 8 fresh mint leaves, plus additional for garnish
- ½ ounce simple syrup (page 6)
- 2 ounces bourbon whiskey

Muddle lemon quarters, 8 mint leaves and simple syrup in cocktail shaker. Add bourbon; shake until blended. Strain into old fashioned glass filled with crushed ice; garnish with additional mint.

NEGRONI >

MAKES 1 SERVING

- 1 ounce gin
- 1 ounce Campari
- 1 ounce sweet vermouth
- Orange slice or twist

Fill cocktail shaker half full with ice; add gin, Campari and vermouth. Stir until blended; strain into old fashioned glass. Garnish with orange slice.

ECLIPSE

MAKES 1 SERVING

- 2 ounces tequila añejo
- ¾ ounce Aperol
- ¾ ounce cherry liqueur
- ¾ ounce lemon juice
- ¼ ounce mezcal
- Lemon twist

Fill cocktail shaker half full with ice; add tequila, Aperol, liqueur, lemon juice and mezcal. Shake until blended; strain into coupe or old fashioned glass. Garnish with lemon twist.

MINT JULEP

MAKES 1 SERVING

- 4 to 6 fresh mint leaves, plus additional for garnish
- 1 teaspoon sugar
- 3 ounces bourbon whiskey

Muddle mint leaves and sugar in old fashioned glass. Fill glass with crushed ice; stir in bourbon. Garnish with additional mint.

VESPER >

MAKES 1 SERVING

- 3 ounces gin
- 1 ounce vodka
- ½ ounce Lillet Blanc
- Lemon twist

Fill cocktail shaker half full with ice; add gin, vodka and Lillet Blanc. Shake until blended; strain into cocktail glass. Garnish with lemon twist.

WHISKEY SOUR

MAKES 1 SERVING

- 2 ounces whiskey
- 1½ ounces lemon juice*
- ½ ounce simple syrup (page 6)*

**Or substitute 2 ounces Homemade Sour Mix (recipe follows) for the lemon juice and simple syrup.*

Fill cocktail shaker half full with ice; add whiskey, lemon juice and simple syrup. Shake until blended; strain into ice-filled old fashioned glass.

HOMEMADE SOUR MIX

Combine 1 cup water and 1 cup sugar in small saucepan. Cook over medium heat just until sugar is dissolved. Pour into glass jar; stir in 1 cup lemon juice and ½ cup lime juice. Cool completely; store in refrigerator.

GODFATHER >

MAKES 1 SERVING

- 1½ ounces Scotch
- ½ ounce amaretto
- Orange slice or twist

Fill mixing glass or cocktail shaker half full with ice; add Scotch and amaretto. Stir 30 seconds or until cold; strain into ice-filled old fashioned glass. Garnish with orange slice.

CLOVER CLUB

MAKES 1 SERVING

- 1½ ounces gin
- ¾ ounce lemon juice
- ½ ounce dry vermouth
- 2 teaspoons grenadine or raspberry syrup
- 1 egg white

Combine gin, lemon juice, vermouth, grenadine and egg white in cocktail shaker; shake 10 seconds without ice. Fill shaker half full with ice; shake about 30 seconds or until cold and frothy. Strain into cocktail glass.

EL DORADO >

MAKES 1 SERVING

- 1 tablespoon honey
- 1 tablespoon boiling water
- 2 ounces tequila
- 1½ ounces lemon juice
- Lemon or orange slice

Dissolve honey in boiling water in cocktail shaker. Fill half full with ice; add tequila and lemon juice. Shake until blended; strain into ice-filled old fashioned or Collins glass. Garnish with lemon slice.

TEQUILA SOUR

MAKES 1 SERVING

- 2 ounces tequila
- 1 ounce lemon juice
- ½ ounce simple syrup (page 6)
- 2 dashes bitters
- 1 egg white (optional)

1. Combine tequila, lemon juice, simple syrup, bitters and egg white, if desired, in cocktail shaker; shake 15 seconds.
2. Fill half full with ice; shake 30 seconds. Strain into glass.

FESTIVE & FRUITY

HURRICANE

MAKES 1 SERVING

- 2 ounces light rum
- 2 ounces dark rum
- 1 ounce passion fruit juice
- 1 ounce orange juice
- 1 ounce lime juice
- ½ ounce grenadine
- Lime slices

Fill cocktail shaker half full with ice; add rums, juices and grenadine. Shake until blended; strain into ice-filled hurricane glass. Garnish with lime slices.

TEQUILA SUNRISE >

MAKES 1 SERVING

- 4 ice cubes
- 2 ounces tequila
- 6 ounces orange juice
- 1 tablespoon grenadine

Place ice cubes in highball glass. Pour tequila and orange juice over ice (do not stir). Pour in grenadine; let sink to bottom of glass. (Do not stir.)

GIMLET

MAKES 1 SERVING

- 2 ounces gin
- 1 ounce lime juice
- 1 ounce simple syrup (page 6)
- Lime wedge

Fill cocktail shaker half full with ice; add gin, lime juice and simple syrup. Shake until blended; strain into cocktail glass. Garnish with lime wedge.

RUM SWIZZLE

MAKES 1 SERVING

- 2 ounces rum
- 1 ounce lime juice
- 1 teaspoon superfine sugar
- 2 dashes Angostura bitters
- Lime slice

Combine rum, lime juice, sugar and bitters in Collins or highball glass filled with crushed ice; stir with long spoon until blended and cold. Garnish with lime slice.

ZOMBIE

MAKES 1 SERVING

- 2 ounces light rum
- 1 ounce dark rum
- 1 ounce lime juice
- 1 ounce pineapple juice
- 1 ounce orange juice or papaya juice
- ½ ounce apricot brandy
- 1 teaspoon superfine sugar or simple syrup (page 6)
- ½ cup crushed ice
- ½ ounce 151-proof rum
- ½ ounce grenadine
- Fresh mint sprig

Fill cocktail shaker half full with ice; add light rum, dark rum, juices, brandy and sugar. Shake until blended; strain into Collins glass filled with crushed ice. Float 151-proof rum and grenadine on top. Garnish with mint.

BLENDED VARIATION

Combine light rum, dark rum, lime juice, pineapple juice, orange juice, brandy, sugar and ½ cup ice in blender; blend until smooth. Pour mixture into Collins or highball glass. Float 151-proof rum and grenadine on top.

APPLE MARTINI >

MAKES 1 SERVING

- 2 ounces vodka
- 1 ounce apple schnapps
- 1 ounce apple juice
- Apple slices

Fill cocktail shaker half full with ice; add vodka, schnapps and apple juice. Shake until blended; strain into cocktail glass. Garnish with apple slices.

SOUR APPLE MARTINI

Substitute sour apple schnapps for apple schnapps.

SEA BREEZE

MAKES 1 SERVING

- 3 ounces cranberry juice
- 2 ounces grapefruit juice
- 1½ ounces vodka
- Lemon slice

Fill cocktail shaker half full with ice; add cranberry juice, grapefruit juice and vodka. Shake until blended; strain into ice-filled Collins or highball glass. Garnish with lemon slice.

PALOMA >

MAKES 1 SERVING

- 1 lime wedge
- Coarse salt
- ¼ cup grapefruit juice
- ½ ounce lime juice
- 1 teaspoon sugar
- 2 ounces tequila
- Ice cubes
- ¼ cup club soda

Rub rim of highball glass with lime wedge; dip in coarse salt. Combine grapefruit juice, lime juice and sugar in glass; stir until sugar is dissolved. Add tequila and ice to fill glass; top with club soda. Garnish with lime wedge.

PIÑA COLADA

MAKES 1 SERVING

- 4 ounces pineapple juice
- 1½ ounces light rum
- 1½ ounces coconut cream
- ½ cup crushed ice
- Pineapple wedge and maraschino cherry

Combine pineapple juice, rum and coconut cream in blender. Add ice; blend 15 seconds or until smooth. Pour into Collins or hurricane glass; garnish with pineapple wedge and maraschino cherry.

GRAPEFRUIT DAIQUIRI >

MAKES 1 SERVING

- 2 ounces grapefruit juice
- 2 ounces light rum
- ½ ounce lime juice
- 1 teaspoon maraschino cherry juice
- Lime slice

Fill cocktail shaker half full with ice; add grapefruit juice, rum, lime juice and maraschino cherry juice. Shake until blended; strain into cocktail glass. Garnish with lime slice.

BAHAMA MAMA

MAKES 1 SERVING

- 2 ounces pineapple juice
- 2 ounces orange juice
- 1 ounce light rum
- 1 ounce gold rum
- 1 ounce dark rum
- 1 ounce coconut liqueur
- ¼ teaspoon grenadine
- Orange slice and maraschino cherry

Fill cocktail shaker half full with ice; add pineapple juice, orange juice, rums, liqueur and grenadine. Shake until blended; strain into hurricane glass. Garnish with orange slice and cherry.

AVIATION >

MAKES 1 SERVING

- 2 ounces gin
- ¾ ounce lemon juice
- ½ ounce maraschino liqueur
- ¼ ounce crème de violette
- Maraschino cherries and lemon twist

Fill cocktail shaker half full with ice; add gin, lemon juice and liqueurs. Shake until blended; strain into cocktail glass. Garnish with cherries and lemon twist.

COCO LOCO

MAKES 1 SERVING

- 4 ounces pineapple juice
- 2 ounces light rum
- 1 ounce cream of coconut
- 1 ounce milk
- ½ ounce amaretto
- 1 teaspoon grenadine
- ½ cup ice cubes

Combine pineapple juice, rum, cream of coconut, milk, amaretto, grenadine and ice in blender; blend until smooth. Pour into wine glass.

MAI TAI >

MAKES 1 SERVING

- 1 ounce light rum
- 1 ounce triple sec
- ½ ounce grenadine
- ½ ounce orgeat syrup*
- ½ ounce lime juice
- 1 ounce dark rum
- Pineapple wedge and maraschino cherry

**Almond-flavored syrup.*

Fill cocktail shaker half full with ice; add light rum, triple sec, grenadine, orgeat syrup and lime juice. Shake until blended; strain into old fashioned glass. Pour dark rum over top (do not stir). Garnish with pineapple wedge and maraschino cherry.

JUNGLE BIRD

MAKES 1 SERVING

- 1½ ounces Jamaican or dark rum
- 1½ ounces pineapple juice
- ¾ ounce Campari
- ½ ounce lime juice
- ½ ounce simple syrup (page 6)
- Pineapple wedge

Fill cocktail shaker with ice; add rum, pineapple juice, Campari, lime juice and simple syrup. Shake 30 seconds or until cold; strain into ice-filled old fashioned glass. Garnish with pineapple wedge.

PITCHERS & PUNCHES

STRAWBERRY-APRICOT PUNCH

MAKES 12 SERVINGS

- 2 packages (10 ounces each) frozen sliced strawberries in syrup, thawed
- 2 cans (5½ ounces each) apricot or peach nectar
- ¼ cup lemon juice
- 2 tablespoons honey
- 1 bottle (2 liters) lemon-lime soda
- Lemon slices and fresh strawberry halves (optional)

1 Place strawberries with syrup in food processor or blender; process until smooth.

2 Pour puréed strawberries into large pitcher or punch bowl. Stir in apricot nectar, lemon juice and honey until well blended. Stir soda into punch just before serving. Float lemon and strawberry halves in punch, if desired.

WHITE SANGRIA >

MAKES 8 TO 10 SERVINGS

- 2 oranges, cut into ¼-inch slices
- 2 lemons, cut into ¼-inch slices
- ½ cup sugar
- 2 bottles (750 ml each) dry white wine
- ½ cup peach schnapps
- 3 ripe peaches, pitted and cut into wedges
- Raspberries and sliced strawberries

1 Place orange and lemon slices in large pitcher or punch bowl. Pour sugar over fruit; mash lightly until sugar dissolves and fruit begins to break down.

2 Stir in wine, schnapps and peaches; mix well. Refrigerate at least 2 hours or overnight. Stir in raspberries and strawberries just before serving.

CUCUMBER PUNCH

MAKES 10 SERVINGS

- 1 seedless cucumber, thinly sliced
- 1 cup water
- 1 can (6 ounces) thawed frozen limeade concentrate
- 1 bottle (2 liters) chilled club soda *or* 2 bottles (750 ml each) sparkling wine
- Lime wedges (optional)

1 Combine cucumber slices, water and limeade concentrate in large pitcher or punch bowl. Refrigerate 1 hour.

2 Stir in club soda just before serving. Serve over ice; garnish with lime wedges.

STRAWBERRY-BASIL SPARKLERS >

MAKES 8 SERVINGS

- 1 cup fresh basil leaves, plus additional for garnish
- ⅔ cup sugar
- ⅔ cup water
- 4 cups fresh strawberries, plus additional for garnish
- 1 bottle (1 liter) cold club soda *or* 1 bottle (750 ml) sparkling wine

1. Combine 1 cup basil, sugar and water in small saucepan; cook and stir over medium heat until sugar is dissolved. Remove from heat; cool completely. Strain through fine-mesh sieve; discard basil. (Syrup can be stored in refrigerator up to 1 week.)
2. Combine 4 cups strawberries and basil syrup in blender; blend until smooth. Pour into pitcher. Stir in club soda just before serving. Serve over ice; garnish with additional strawberries and basil.

CARIBBEAN RUM PUNCH

MAKES 10 SERVINGS

- 2 cups pineapple juice
- 2 cups orange juice
- 2 cups grenadine
- 2 cups dark rum
- 1 cup coconut rum
- 1 cup lime juice (about 8 limes)
- 6 to 8 drops Angostura bitters
- Orange slices and pineapple wedges

1. Combine juices, grenadine, rums, lime juice and bitters in large pitcher; mix well. Refrigerate until ready to serve.
2. Serve over ice; garnish with orange slices and pineapple wedges.

CUBAN GUAVA PUNCH >

MAKES 8 SERVINGS

- 2 cups water
- ¾ cup sugar
- 1½ cups chilled guava nectar
- 1½ cups chilled orange juice
- 4 ounces chilled pineapple juice
- 2 ounces lime juice

1 Combine water and sugar in small saucepan; cook and stir over medium heat until sugar dissolves. Cool to room temperature; pour into large pitcher.

2 Stir in guava nectar, orange juice, pineapple juice and lime juice; mix well. Serve over ice.

BLENDED MANGO RUM PUNCH

MAKES 4 SERVINGS

- 2 cups ice cubes
- 1 cup mango juice
- 4 ounces triple sec
- 2 ounces dark rum
- 2 tablespoons lime juice
- 1 tablespoon sugar

Combine ice, mango juice, triple sec, rum, lime juice and sugar in blender; blend until smooth. Pour into four glasses; serve immediately.

APPLE-BERRY PUNCH >

MAKES ABOUT 10 SERVINGS

- 8 to 12 medium fresh strawberries *or* 30 fresh red raspberries
- 7 cups apple juice, divided
- 1 (4-inch) cinnamon stick, broken
- ½ teaspoon whole allspice
- ½ teaspoon vanilla
- 2 cans (12 ounces each) chilled lemon-lime soda or ginger ale *or* 1 bottle (750 ml) sparkling wine

1 Cut strawberries in half. Place one strawberry half in each section of three ice cube trays. Spoon about 1 tablespoon apple juice over each piece of fruit. Freeze until firm.

2 Tie cinnamon and allspice in cheesecloth bag. Combine spice bag and remaining apple juice in large saucepan; bring to a boil. Reduce heat to low; cover and simmer 5 minutes. Remove from heat; stir in vanilla. Cover and refrigerate 6 hours or until cold.

3 Remove spice bag from apple juice mixture; discard. Pour into large pitcher or small punch bowl. Gently stir in soda. Float frozen apple juice cubes in punch.

ROSÉ SANGRIA

MAKES 8 SERVINGS

- ½ cup sugar
- 2 ounces water
- 2 bottles (750 ml each) rosé wine
- 8 ounces orange juice
- 2 ounces lemon juice
- 1 orange, thinly sliced
- 1 lemon, thinly sliced

1 Combine sugar and water in small saucepan; cook and stir over medium heat just until sugar is dissolved. Pour into large pitcher. Add wine, orange juice, lemon juice and orange and lemon slices; cover and refrigerate at least 2 hours for flavors to blend.

2 Serve sangria over ice.

WINE, BEER & BUBBLES

< BICICLETTA

MAKES 1 DRINK

- 3 ounces dry white wine
- 2 ounces Campari
- Chilled club soda or soda water

Fill old-fashioned glass with ice; add wine and Campari. Fill with club soda; stir gently to mix.

QUICK MICHELADA

MAKES 1 SERVING

- 1 lime wedge
- Coarse salt
- ¼ cup ice cubes
- 2 ounces lime juice
- 1 bottle (12 ounces) chilled Mexican beer (use ¾ of bottle)
- Hot pepper sauce (optional)

Rub rim of large beer glass with lime wedge; dip in salt to coat rim. Add ice and lime juice to glass; add enough beer to fill glass. Stir in hot pepper sauce, if desired.

SNAKE BITE >

MAKES 1 SERVING

- **8 ounces chilled ale**
- **8 ounces chilled hard cider**

Pour ale into pint glass; top with cider. (Do not stir.)

CRAN-RASPBERRY SPRITZER

MAKES 1 SERVING

- **2 ounces chilled cranberry juice**
- **½ ounce chilled raspberry vodka**
- **6 ounces chilled sparkling wine**

Combine cranberry juice and vodka in champagne flute; top with sparkling wine.

BELLINI >

MAKES 1 SERVING

- 3 ounces peach nectar*
- 4 ounces chilled champagne or dry sparkling wine

**Or peel and pit a ripe medium peach and purée in blender.*

Pour peach nectar into champagne flute; slowly pour in champagne and stir gently.

GRAPEFRUIT RADLER

MAKES 1 SERVING

- 4 ounces grapefruit juice
- 1 teaspoon sugar
- 1 bottle (12 ounces) chilled wheat beer
- Chilled grapefruit seltzer or soda water (optional)

Combine grapefruit juice and sugar in large glass; stir to dissolve sugar. Add beer; stir gently to mix. Top with soda, if desired.

SUMMER BEER >

MAKES 8 SERVINGS

- Ice cubes
- 4 bottles (12 ounces each) chilled pilsner or lager beer
- 1 can (12 ounces) frozen lemonade concentrate
- 12 ounces vodka or rum
- Lemon slices and mint leaves

Fill pitcher half full with ice. Add beer, lemonade concentrate and vodka; mix gently until blended. Garnish with lemon slices and mint.

NEGRONI SBAGLIATO

MAKES 1 SERVING

- 1 ounce sweet vermouth
- 1 ounce Campari
- 1 ounce chilled prosecco

Fill old-fashioned glass with ice; add vermouth and Campari. Top with prosecco; stir gently.

KIR >

MAKES 1 SERVING

- ½ ounce crème de cassis (black currant liqueur)
- 6 ounces chilled dry white wine

Fill old fashioned glass with ice. Pour crème de cassis over ice; top with wine.

KIR ROYALE

Replace white wine with chilled champagne or sparkling wine; serve in champagne glass.

FRENCH 75

MAKES 1 SERVING

- 2 ounces gin
- ½ ounce lemon juice
- 1 teaspoon superfine sugar
- 2 ounces chilled champagne or sparkling wine

Fill cocktail shaker half full with ice; add gin, lemon juice and sugar. Shake until cold; strain into champagne flute or coupe. Top with champagne; stir gently.

MOONWALK >

MAKES 1 SERVING

- 1 ounce grapefruit juice
- 1 ounce triple sec
- 3 drops rosewater*
- Chilled champagne or sparkling wine

**Rosewater can be found at many liquor stores and supermarkets as well as Middle Eastern grocery stores.*

Fill cocktail shaker half full with ice; add grapefruit juice, triple sec and rosewater. Shake until blended; strain into champagne flute. Top with champagne.

SWEET RUBY

MAKES 1 SERVING

- 1 ounce ruby port
- ¾ ounce amaretto
- 2 dashes Angostura bitters

Fill mixing glass or cocktail shaker half full with ice; add port, amaretto and bitters. Stir 10 seconds; strain into chilled old fashioned glass half full with ice.

CUBAN BEER SPRITZER >

MAKES 4 TO 6 SERVINGS

- 3 cups (24 ounces) chilled beer (pilsner or pale ale)
- 3 cups (24 ounces) chilled ginger ale
- 4 ounces lime juice
- ⅓ cup sugar
- 2 cups crushed ice
- Lime slices

Combine beer, ginger ale, lime juice and sugar in large pitcher; stir until sugar dissolves. Divide ice among glasses; pour spritzer over ice. Garnish with lime slices.

SHANDY

MAKES 1 SERVING

- 6 ounces chilled beer
- 6 ounces chilled carbonated lemonade or grapefruit soda
- Lemon slice

Pour beer into large wine glass or pint glass; top with lemonade. Garnish with lemon slice.

SHERRY COBBLER

MAKES 1 SERVING

- ½ teaspoon triple sec
- ½ teaspoon simple syrup (page 6)
- 4 ounces dry sherry (amontillado or oloroso)
- Orange slice

Fill large wine glass or old fashioned glass three-fourths full with crushed ice. Add liqueur and simple syrup; stir until blended. Stir in sherry; garnish with orange slice.

BREAD BITES & TOPPED TOASTS

SPINACH AND FETA STUFFED CHEESY BREAD

MAKES ABOUT 8 SERVINGS

- **1½ cups (6 ounces) shredded mozzarella or Monterey Jack cheese, divided**
- **4 ounces crumbled feta cheese**
- **¼ cup plus 1 tablespoon grated Parmesan cheese, divided**
- **1 teaspoon minced garlic**
- **1 container (11 ounces) refrigerated French bread dough**
- **1 cup baby spinach**
- **½ cup (2 ounces) shredded Cheddar cheese**
- **¼ teaspoon Italian seasoning or dried parsley flakes**

1. Preheat oven to 350°F. Line baking sheet with parchment paper.
2. Combine 1 cup mozzarella, feta, ¼ cup Parmesan and garlic in small bowl; mix well. Unroll dough on prepared baking sheet with long side facing you. Spread half of cheese mixture lengthwise over half of dough; top with spinach and remaining half of cheese mixture. Fold dough in half over filling; press long edge gently to seal.
3. Cut crosswise into 1-inch slices from sealed edge, leaving attached at folded edge (do not separate slices). Top with Cheddar, then remaining ½ cup mozzarella. Sprinkle with Italian seasoning.
4. Bake 25 to 30 minutes or until golden brown. Cut into slices; serve warm.

GARLIC KNOTS

MAKES 20 KNOTS

- 1 package (¼ ounce) instant or rapid-rise active dry yeast
- 1 teaspoon sugar
- ¾ cup warm water (105° to 115°F)
- 2¼ cups all-purpose flour
- 2 tablespoons olive oil, divided
- 1½ teaspoons salt, divided
- 4 tablespoons (½ stick) butter, divided
- 1 tablespoon minced garlic
- ¼ teaspoon garlic powder
- ½ cup grated Parmesan cheese
- 2 tablespoons chopped fresh parsley
- ½ teaspoon dried oregano

1. Dissolve yeast and sugar in warm water in large bowl of stand mixer; let stand 5 minutes or until bubbly. Add flour, 1 tablespoon oil and 1 teaspoon salt; mix with dough hook at low speed 5 minutes or until dough is smooth and elastic.
2. Shape dough into a ball. Place dough in greased bowl; turn to grease top. Cover and let rise in warm place 1 hour or until doubled in size.
3. Melt 2 tablespoons butter in small saucepan over low heat. Add remaining 1 tablespoon oil, ½ teaspoon salt, minced garlic and garlic powder; cook over very low heat 5 minutes. Pour into small bowl; set aside.
4. Preheat oven to 400°F. Line baking sheet with parchment paper.
5. Punch down dough. Turn out dough onto lightly floured surface; let rest 10 minutes. Roll out dough into 10×8-inch rectangle; cut into 20 (2-inch) squares. Roll each piece into 8-inch rope; tie in a knot. Place knots on prepared baking sheet; brush with butter mixture.
6. Bake 10 minutes or until lightly browned. Meanwhile, melt remaining 2 tablespoons butter. Combine cheese, parsley and oregano in small bowl; mix well. Brush melted butter over knots immediately after baking; sprinkle with cheese mixture. Cool slightly; serve warm.

SPINACH FLORENTINE FLATBREAD

MAKES 8 SERVINGS

- 1 tablespoon olive oil
- 2 cloves garlic, minced
- 1 package (10 ounces) baby spinach
- 1 can (about 14 ounces) quartered artichoke hearts, drained and sliced
- ½ teaspoon salt
- ¼ teaspoon dried oregano
- Pinch black pepper
- Pinch red pepper flakes
- 2 rectangular pizza or flatbread crusts (about 8 ounces each)
- 1 plum tomato, seeded and diced
- 2 cups (8 ounces) shredded Monterey Jack cheese
- ½ cup (2 ounces) shredded Italian cheese blend
- Shredded fresh basil leaves (optional)

1. Preheat oven to 425°F.
2. Heat oil in large skillet over medium-high heat. Add garlic; cook and stir 30 seconds. Add half of spinach; cook and stir until slightly wilted. Add additional spinach by handfuls; cook 3 minutes or until completely wilted, stirring occasionally. Remove to medium bowl; stir in artichokes, salt, oregano, black pepper and red pepper flakes.
3. Place pizza crusts on large baking sheet. Spread spinach mixture over crusts; sprinkle with tomato, Monterey Jack cheese and Italian cheese blend.
4. Bake 12 minutes or until cheese is melted and edges of crusts are browned. Garnish with basil.

TIP

For crispier crusts, bake flatbreads on a preheated pizza stone or directly on the oven rack.

PRETZEL MONKEY BREAD

MAKES 12 SERVINGS

- 2½ cups all-purpose flour
- 1½ teaspoons instant or rapid-rise active dry yeast
- 1 teaspoon sugar
- ¼ teaspoon salt
- ¾ cup warm water (120°F)
- 6 tablespoons (¾ stick) butter, melted
- 12 cups water
- ½ cup baking soda
- Coarse salt

DIPPING SAUCE

- 6 tablespoons sour cream
- 2 tablespoons Dijon mustard
- 1 tablespoon honey

1. Combine flour, yeast, sugar and ¼ teaspoon salt in large bowl of stand mixer. Stir in ¾ cup water and 2 tablespoons melted butter to form rough dough. Knead with dough hook at low speed 5 to 7 minutes or until dough is smooth and elastic. Shape dough into a ball. Place dough in greased bowl; turn to grease top. Cover; let rise in warm place about 1 hour or until doubled in size.
2. Preheat oven to 400°F. Line baking sheet with foil. Brush 9-inch springform pan with 1 tablespoon butter; place on prepared baking sheet. Spray outside of 6-ounce ramekin with nonstick cooking spray; place in center of pan. Turn out dough onto lightly floured surface; pat and stretch into 12×6-inch rectangle. Cut dough into 1-inch pieces.
3. Bring 12 cups water to a boil in large saucepan; add baking soda. Working in batches, add dough pieces to boiling water; cook 30 seconds. Place half of hot dough pieces around ramekin in prepared pan; brush with half of remaining butter and sprinkle with coarse salt. Top with remaining dough pieces; brush with remaining butter and sprinkle with coarse salt.
4. Bake about 30 minutes or until pretzels are dark golden brown. Loosen edges of bread with knife; carefully remove side of pan.
5. For dipping sauce, combine sour cream, mustard and honey in small bowl. Carefully remove hot ramekin from center of pretzel ring and replace with bowl of sauce. (Ramekin from oven will be too hot for sauce.) Serve warm.

BALSAMIC ONION AND PROSCIUTTO PIZZETTES

MAKES 16 PIZZETTES

- **1 package (16 ounces) refrigerated pizza dough***
- **2 tablespoons olive oil, divided**
- **1 large *or* 2 small red onions, cut in half and thinly sliced**
- **¼ teaspoon salt**
- **1½ tablespoons balsamic vinegar**
- **⅛ teaspoon black pepper**
- **⅔ cup grated Parmesan cheese**
- **4 ounces fresh mozzarella, cut into small pieces**
- **1 package (about 3 ounces) thinly sliced prosciutto, cut or torn into small pieces**

Or use frozen pizza dough; thaw according to package directions.

1 Remove dough from refrigerator; let stand at room temperature while preparing onions. Heat 1 tablespoon oil in medium skillet over medium-high heat. Add onion and salt; cook about 20 minutes or until tender and golden brown, stirring occasionally. Add vinegar and pepper; cook and stir 2 minutes. Remove from heat.

2 Preheat oven to 450°F. Line two baking sheets with parchment paper.

3 Divide dough into 16 balls; press into 3-inch rounds (about ⅜ inch thick) on prepared baking sheets. Brush rounds with remaining 1 tablespoon oil; sprinkle each with about 1 teaspoon Parmesan. Top with cooked onion, mozzarella, prosciutto and remaining Parmesan.

4 Bake about 13 minutes or until crusts are golden brown.

CROSTINI WITH EGGPLANT TAPENADE

MAKES 8 SERVINGS

- **3 tablespoons olive oil**
- **2 cups diced eggplant**
- **½ cup chopped shallots or onion**
- **1 cup pitted kalamata olives, chopped**
- **½ cup red peppadew peppers, chopped with 2 tablespoons juice***
- **1 tablespoon drained capers**
- **½ cup cola beverage**
- **1 tablespoon balsamic vinegar**
- **½ teaspoon red pepper flakes**
- **Salt and black pepper**
- **Toasted baguette slices**

****If peppadew peppers are unavailable, substitute chopped roasted red peppers.***

1 Heat oil in large nonstick skillet over medium-high heat. Add eggplant and shallots; cook about 6 minutes or until golden brown, stirring often. Add olives, peppadew peppers with juice and capers; cook and stir 5 minutes or until most liquid has evaporated.

2 Stir in cola, vinegar, red pepper flakes; season to taste with salt and black pepper. Reduce heat to low; cook about 15 minutes or until thickened, stirring occasionally. Serve warm or at room temperature on baguette slices.

PEPPERONI BREAD

MAKES ABOUT 6 SERVINGS

- 1 package (about 14 ounces) refrigerated pizza dough
- 8 slices provolone cheese
- 20 to 30 slices pepperoni (about half of 6-ounce package)
- ½ teaspoon Italian seasoning
- ¾ cup (3 ounces) shredded mozzarella cheese
- ½ cup grated Parmesan cheese
- 1 egg, beaten
- Marinara sauce, heated

1. Preheat oven to 400°F. Unroll pizza dough on sheet of parchment paper with long side facing you.
2. Arrange half of provolone slices over bottom half dough, cutting to fit as necessary. Top with pepperoni; sprinkle with ¼ teaspoon Italian seasoning. Top with mozzarella, Parmesan and remaining provolone slices; sprinkle with remaining ¼ teaspoon Italian seasoning.
3. Fold top half of dough over filling; press edges with fork or pinch edges to seal. Transfer bread on parchment paper to large baking sheet. Brush with beaten egg.
4. Bake 16 minutes or until crust is golden brown. Remove to wire rack to cool slightly. Cut crosswise into slices; serve with marinara sauce.

TUSCAN WHITE BEAN CROSTINI

MAKES 18 CROSTINI

- ⅓ cup red wine vinegar
- 3 tablespoons chopped fresh parsley
- 1 tablespoon olive oil
- 2 cloves garlic, minced
- ½ teaspoon salt
- ½ teaspoon dried oregano
- ¼ teaspoon black pepper
- 2 cans (about 15 ounces each) cannellini or Great Northern beans, rinsed and drained
- ½ red bell pepper, finely chopped *or* ⅓ cup finely chopped roasted red pepper
- ⅓ cup finely chopped onion
- 18 slices French bread, about ¼ inch thick

1 Whisk vinegar, parsley, oil, garlic, salt, oregano and black pepper in large bowl until well blended. Stir in beans, bell pepper and onion. Cover and refrigerate 2 hours or overnight.

2 Preheat broiler. Arrange bread slices in single layer on large baking sheet or broiler pan. Broil 6 to 8 inches from heat 30 to 45 seconds or until lightly toasted. Cool completely. Serve bean mixture on toasts.

PULL-APART GARLIC CHEESE BREAD

MAKES 12 SERVINGS

- 3 cups all-purpose flour
- 1 package (¼ ounce) instant or rapid-rise active dry yeast
- 1 teaspoon salt
- 1 cup warm water (120°F)
- 2 tablespoons olive oil
- 6 cloves garlic, minced, divided
- ¼ cup (½ stick) butter
- ¼ teaspoon paprika
- 1 cup grated Parmesan cheese
- 1 cup (4 ounces) shredded mozzarella cheese
- ½ cup pizza sauce
- Chopped fresh parsley (optional)

1. Combine flour, yeast and salt in large bowl of stand mixer. Stir in water and oil with wooden spoon to form rough dough. Add half of garlic; mix with dough hook at low speed 5 to 7 minutes or until dough is smooth and elastic.
2. Shape dough into a ball. Place in greased bowl; turn to grease top. Cover and let rise in warm place 45 minutes to 1 hour or until doubled in size.
3. Line baking sheet with foil. Brush 9-inch springform pan with some of butter mixture; place on prepared baking sheet. Place 6-ounce ramekin in center of pan.
4. Melt butter in small skillet over medium-low heat. Add remaining garlic; cook and stir 1 minute. Stir in paprika; remove from heat. Place Parmesan in shallow bowl.
5. Turn out dough onto lightly floured surface; pat into 9-inch square. Cut into 1-inch squares; roll each square into a ball. Dip half of balls in melted butter mixture; roll in Parmesan to coat. Place around ramekin in prepared pan; sprinkle with ½ cup mozzarella. Repeat with remaining dough, butter mixture, Parmesan and mozzarella. Cover and let rise in warm place 1 hour or until dough has risen to top of pan.
6. Preheat oven to 350°F. Pour pizza sauce into ramekin.
7. Bake 20 to 25 minutes or until bread is firm and golden brown. Loosen edges of bread with knife; carefully remove side of pan. Sprinkle with parsley, if desired. Serve warm.

FRENCH-STYLE PIZZA BITES

MAKES ABOUT 24 SERVINGS

- 2 tablespoons olive oil
- 1 onion, thinly sliced
- 1 red bell pepper, cut into 3-inch-long strips
- 2 cloves garlic, minced
- ⅓ cup pitted black olives, cut into thin wedges
- 1 package (about 14 ounces) refrigerated pizza dough
- ¾ cup (3 ounces) finely shredded Swiss or Gruyère cheese

1. Preheat oven to 425°F. Grease large baking sheet.
2. Heat oil in medium skillet over medium heat. Add onion, bell pepper and garlic; cook and stir 5 minutes or until crisp-tender. Stir in olives. Remove from heat; set aside.
3. Pat dough into 16×12-inch rectangle on prepared baking sheet. Arrange onion mixture over dough; sprinkle with cheese. Bake 10 minutes. Loosen crust with long spatula; slide onto oven rack. Bake 3 to 5 minutes more or until golden brown.
4. Slide baking sheet under crust and remove crust from rack. Transfer to cutting board. Cut pizza crosswise into eight 1¾-inch-wide strips; cut diagonally into ten 2-inch-wide strips, making diamond pieces.

BEANS AND GREENS CROSTINI

MAKES ABOUT 24 CROSTINI

- 4 tablespoons olive oil, divided
- 1 onion, thinly sliced
- 4 cups thinly sliced Italian black kale or other dinosaur kale variety
- 2 tablespoons minced garlic, divided
- 1 tablespoon balsamic vinegar
- 2 teaspoons salt, divided
- ¼ teaspoon red pepper flakes
- 1 can (about 15 ounces) cannellini beans, rinsed and drained
- 1 tablespoon chopped fresh rosemary
- Toasted baguette slices

1. Heat 1 tablespoon oil in large skillet over medium heat. Add onion; cook and stir 5 minutes or until softened. Add kale and 1 tablespoon garlic; cook 15 minutes or until kale is softened and most liquid has evaporated, stirring occasionally. Stir in vinegar, 1 teaspoon salt and red pepper flakes.
2. Meanwhile, combine beans, remaining 3 tablespoons oil, 1 tablespoon garlic, 1 teaspoon salt and rosemary in food processor or blender; process until smooth.
3. Spread baguette slices with bean mixture; top with kale.

CLASSIC TOMATO BRUSCHETTA

MAKES 4 SERVINGS

- 1 tablespoon olive oil
- ½ clove garlic, minced
- 2 cups chopped seeded tomatoes (3 medium)
- ⅛ teaspoon salt
- Black pepper
- Toasted Italian bread slices
- 2 tablespoons slivered fresh basil (optional)

1 Preheat oven to 350°F. Heat oil and garlic in small skillet over medium heat 2 minutes, stirring occasionally. Remove from heat; transfer to medium bowl. Stir in tomatoes, salt and pepper; mix well.

2 Place bread slices on baking sheet. Bake 8 to 10 minutes or until golden brown. Cool slightly. Top with tomato mixture and basil, if desired.

MOZZARELLA IN CARROZZA

MAKES ABOUT 8 APPETIZER SERVINGS

- 2 eggs
- ⅓ cup milk
- ¼ teaspoon salt
- ⅛ teaspoon black pepper
- 8 slices country Italian bread
- 8 to 12 fresh basil leaves, torn
- 8 oil-packed sun-dried tomatoes, drained and cut into strips
- 6 ounces fresh mozzarella, cut into ¼-inch slices
- 1½ tablespoons olive oil

1. Whisk eggs, milk, salt and pepper in shallow bowl or baking dish until well blended.
2. Place four bread slices on work surface. Top with basil, sun-dried tomatoes, cheese and remaining bread slices.
3. Heat oil in large skillet over medium heat. Dip sandwiches in egg mixture, turning and pressing to coat completely. Add sandwiches to skillet; cook 5 minutes per side or until golden brown. Cut into strips or squares.

PARMESAN GARLIC MONKEY BREAD

MAKES 12 SERVINGS

- 3 tablespoons butter, melted
- 3 tablespoons olive oil
- 2 teaspoons garlic powder
- 2 teaspoons Italian seasoning
- 2 cups grated Parmesan cheese (do not use shredded)
- 1 container (about 16 ounces) refrigerated jumbo biscuits (8 biscuits)
- 1 container (about 10 ounces) refrigerated jumbo biscuits (5 biscuits)
- Pizza sauce or marinara sauce (optional)

1. Preheat oven to 350°F. Spray 12-cup (10-inch) bundt pan generously with nonstick cooking spray.
2. Combine butter, oil, garlic powder and Italian seasoning in medium bowl; mix well. Place cheese in shallow dish.
3. Separate biscuits; cut each biscuit into quarters. Coat each biscuit piece lightly with butter mixture; roll in cheese to coat. Layer biscuit pieces in prepared pan.
4. Bake about 40 minutes or until golden brown. Loosen edges with small knife, if necessary; invert onto serving plate. Serve warm with pizza sauce, if desired.

BEAN AND SPINACH BRUSCHETTA

MAKES 16 SERVINGS

- **1 can (about 15 ounces) Great Northern or cannellini beans, rinsed and drained**
- **¼ cup grated Parmesan cheese**
- **½ teaspoon onion powder**
- **4 tablespoons olive oil, divided**
- **2 cloves garlic, minced**
- **½ teaspoon salt, divided**
- **½ teaspoon black pepper, divided**
- **6 cups spinach, loosely packed, finely chopped**
- **1 tablespoon red wine vinegar**
- **16 slices whole grain baguette**

1 Purée beans, Parmesan and onion powder in food processor. (If necessary, add 1 to 2 tablespoons water for smoother texture.) Remove to medium bowl.

2 Heat 1 tablespoon oil in medium skillet. Add garlic; cook and stir 1 minute. Remove from heat; add ¼ teaspoon salt and ¼ teaspoon pepper. Stir into beans.

3 Heat 1 tablespoon oil in same skillet over medium heat. Add spinach; cook 2 to 3 minutes or until wilted. Stir in vinegar, remaining ¼ teaspoon salt and ¼ teaspoon pepper. Remove from heat.

4 Preheat grill or broiler. Brush baguette slices with remaining 2 tablespoons oil. Grill until bread is golden brown and crisp. Top with bean purée and spinach.

SOCCA (NIÇOISE CHICKPEA PANCAKE)

MAKES 8 SERVINGS

- 1 cup chickpea flour
- ¾ teaspoon salt
- ½ teaspoon black pepper
- 1 cup water
- 5 tablespoons olive oil, divided
- 1½ teaspoons minced fresh basil *or* ½ teaspoon dried basil
- 1 teaspoon minced fresh rosemary *or* ¼ teaspoon dried rosemary
- ¼ teaspoon dried thyme

1. Sift chickpea flour into medium bowl; stir in salt and pepper. Gradually whisk in water until smooth. Stir in 2 tablespoons oil. Let stand at least 30 minutes.
2. Preheat oven to 450°F. Place 9- or 10-inch cast iron skillet in oven to heat.
3. Add basil, rosemary and thyme to batter; whisk until smooth. Carefully remove skillet from oven. Add 2 tablespoons oil to skillet, swirling to coat pan evenly. Immediately pour in batter.
4. Bake 12 to 15 minutes or until edge of pancake begins to pull away from side of pan and center is firm. Remove from oven. Preheat broiler.
5. Brush with remaining 1 tablespoon oil. Broil 2 to 4 minutes or until dark brown in spots. Cut into wedges. Serve warm.

SPANISH HAM AND CHEESE TOASTS

MAKES 24 SERVINGS

- ½ (11-ounce) package goat cheese, at room temperature
- 1 teaspoon ground cumin
- ½ teaspoon smoked paprika or paprika
- 24 (½-inch) toasted French bread slices
- ½ cup chopped fresh parsley
- 8 slices Serrano ham or prosciutto, cut crosswise into thirds

1 Place goat cheese in small bowl. Add cumin and paprika; stir until well blended and uniform in color. Cover and let stand 30 minutes.

2 Spread goat cheese mixture on bread slices; sprinkle with parsley. Top each toast with one piece of ham. Serve at room temperature.

TIP

Goat cheese mixture can be prepared up to 2 days in advance. This will allow plenty of time for the flavors to blend. For the best flavor, remove goat cheese mixture from the refrigerator 30 minutes before assembling the toasts.

GRILLED CHEESE KABOBS >

MAKES 12 SERVINGS

- **8 thick slices whole wheat bread**
- **4 thick slices sharp Cheddar cheese**
- **3 thick slices Monterey Jack or Colby Jack cheese**
- **2 tablespoons butter, melted**

1. Cut each slice of bread and each slice of cheese into 1-inch squares. Make small sandwiches with one square of bread and one square of each type of cheese. Top with second square of bread.
2. Brush four sides of sandwiches with melted butter. Heat nonstick grill pan or skillet over medium-high heat. Cook sandwich kabobs 30 seconds on each of 4 sides or until golden and cheese is slightly melted. Remove sandwiches from skillet with short wooden skewers.

MARGHERITA CROSTINI

MAKES 8 SERVINGS

- **1 whole wheat mini baguette (about 4 ounces)**
- **4 plum tomatoes**
- **1 cup (4 ounces) shredded mozzarella cheese**
- **3 tablespoons pesto sauce**

1. Preheat oven to 400°F. Slice baguette into 16 very thin diagonal slices. Slice each tomato lengthwise into 4 (¼-inch) slices.
2. Place baguette slices on ungreased baking sheet. Top each with 1 tablespoon cheese and 1 tomato slice.
3. Bake 8 minutes or until bread is lightly toasted and cheese is melted. Top each crostini with about ½ teaspoon pesto sauce. Serve warm.

PARMESAN AND PINE NUT SHORTBREAD >

MAKES 26 TO 28 COOKIES

- ½ cup all-purpose flour
- ⅓ cup whole wheat flour
- ⅓ cup cornmeal
- ¼ teaspoon salt
- ½ cup (1 stick) butter, softened
- ½ cup shredded Parmesan cheese
- ⅓ cup sugar
- 3 to 5 tablespoons pine nuts

1 Whisk flours, cornmeal and salt in small bowl.

2 Beat butter, cheese and sugar in medium bowl with electric mixer at high speed until light and fluffy. Gradually add flour mixture to butter, beating at low speed after each addition. Transfer dough to work surface; shape into log 8 to 10 inches long and about 2 inches in diameter. Wrap in plastic wrap and chill 30 minutes.

3 Preheat oven to 375°F. Line baking sheet with parchment paper. Cut dough into ⅓-inch slices with sharp knife. Arrange 1 inch apart on prepared baking sheet. Press 3 to 5 pine nuts on each slice. Bake 11 to 13 minutes or until firm and lightly browned. Cool on baking sheet 5 minutes. Remove to wire rack; cool completely.

HOT PEPPER CRANBERRY JELLY APPETIZER

MAKES 16 SERVINGS

- ½ cup whole berry cranberry sauce
- ¼ cup apricot fruit spread
- 1 teaspoon sugar
- 1 teaspoon cider vinegar
- ½ teaspoon red pepper flakes
- ½ teaspoon grated fresh ginger
- Crackers and sliced cheeses

1 Combine cranberry sauce, fruit spread, sugar, vinegar and red pepper flakes in small saucepan. Cook over medium heat just until sugar is dissolved. Transfer to bowl; cool completely. Stir in ginger.

2 Top crackers with cheese slices and cranberry mixture.

NUTS & NIBBLES

CHOCOLATE-ALMOND CRISPY TREATS

MAKES 2 TO 3 DOZEN BARS

- **6 cups crisp brown rice cereal**
- **1½ cups sliced almonds, toasted***
- **1 cup light corn syrup**
- **⅓ cup almond butter**
- **¼ cup packed brown sugar**
- **3 tablespoons unsweetened cocoa powder**
- **¼ teaspoon salt**
- **1 cup semisweet chocolate chips**

****To toast almonds, spread in single layer in heavy skillet. Cook over medium heat 1 to 2 minutes or until nuts are lightly browned, stirring frequently.***

1 Line 13×9-inch baking pan with parchment paper; spray with nonstick cooking spray.

2 Combine cereal and almonds in large bowl.

3 Combine corn syrup, almond butter, brown sugar, cocoa and salt in large saucepan; cook and stir over medium heat 5 minutes or until mixture is smooth and just begins to boil across surface. Remove from heat.

4 Immediately stir cereal mixture into saucepan. Gently fold in chocolate chips. Press firmly into prepared pan. Let stand 1 hour or until set. Cut into bars.

SOUTHWEST SNACK MIX

MAKES 6 CUPS

- 4 cups corn cereal squares
- 2 cups pretzel twists
- ½ cup pumpkin seeds (pepitas)
- 1½ teaspoons chili powder
- 1 teaspoon minced fresh cilantro or parsley
- ½ teaspoon garlic powder
- ½ teaspoon onion powder
- 1 egg white
- 2 tablespoons olive oil
- 2 tablespoons lime juice

1. Preheat oven to 300°F. Spray baking sheet with nonstick cooking spray.
2. Combine cereal, pretzels and pumpkin seeds in large bowl. Combine chili powder, cilantro, garlic powder and onion powder in small bowl.
3. Whisk egg white, oil and lime juice in separate small bowl until well blended. Pour over cereal mixture; toss to coat. Add seasoning mixture; mix lightly to coat evenly. Spread on prepared baking sheet.
4. Bake 45 minutes, stirring every 15 minutes. Cool completely. Store in airtight container.

VARIATION

Substitute ½ cup peanuts for pumpkin seeds.

CRUNCHY RAMEN CHOW

MAKES ABOUT 8 CUPS

- **4 packages (3 ounces each) ramen noodles***
- **1 cup semisweet chocolate chips**
- **1 cup butterscotch chips**
- **¾ cup creamy peanut butter**
- **¼ cup (½ stick) butter**
- **1½ cups powdered sugar**

****Use any flavor; discard seasoning packets.***

1. Line large baking sheet with parchment or waxed paper. Break noodles into bite-size pieces; place in large bowl.
2. Combine chocolate chips, butterscotch chips, peanut butter and butter in large microwavable bowl. Microwave on HIGH 1 minute; stir. Continue heating and stirring at 30-second intervals until melted and smooth.
3. Pour chocolate mixture over noodles; stir to coat evenly. Transfer to large resealable food storage bag.
4. Add powdered sugar to bag; seal bag. Shake until well coated. Spread in single layer on prepared baking sheet; let stand until set. Store in airtight container.

PARMESAN RANCH SNACK MIX

MAKES ABOUT 9½ CUPS

- 3 cups corn or rice cereal squares
- 2 cups oyster crackers
- 1 package (5 ounces) bagel chips, broken in half
- 1½ cups mini pretzel twists
- 1 cup shelled pistachio nuts
- 2 tablespoons grated Parmesan cheese
- ¼ cup (½ stick) butter, melted
- 1 package (1 ounce) dry ranch salad dressing mix
- ½ teaspoon garlic powder

SLOW COOKER DIRECTIONS

1. Combine cereal, oyster crackers, bagel chips, pretzels, pistachios and cheese in slow cooker; mix gently.
2. Combine butter, salad dressing mix and garlic powder in small bowl. Pour over cereal mixture; toss lightly to coat. Cover; cook on LOW 3 hours.
3. Remove cover; stir gently. Cook, uncovered, on LOW 30 minutes.

PRETZEL CANDY CLUSTERS

MAKES ABOUT 5 CUPS

- **6 squares (2 ounces each) white almond bark, chopped, divided**
- **1½ cups pretzel sticks**
- **Orange food coloring (optional)**
- **2 cups graham cereal**
- **¾ cup candy-coated chocolate pieces**
- **¾ cup mini marshmallows**
- **½ cup chocolate sprinkles**

1. Line two baking sheets with parchment paper.
2. Place 1½ squares almond bark in small microwavable bowl. Microwave on MEDIUM (50%) 1 minute; stir. Continue heating and stirring at 15-second intervals until melted and smooth.
3. Place pretzel sticks in large bowl. Stir in melted almond bark until all pieces are coated. Spread on prepared baking sheet, separating individual pieces; let stand until set.
4. Place remaining 4½ squares almond bark in medium microwavable bowl. Microwave on MEDIUM (50%) 1 minute; stir. Continue heating and stirring at 15-second intervals until melted and smooth. If desired, stir in food coloring one drop at a time until desired orange color is reached.
5. Place cereal in large bowl. Stir in half of melted orange almond bark until cereal is evenly coated. Stir in chocolate pieces, marshmallows and remaining almond bark. Stir in pretzel sticks.
6. Scoop mixture into small clusters on prepared baking sheet. Sprinkle with chocolate sprinkles; let stand until set.

CHOCO-PEANUT BUTTER POPCORN >

MAKES 4 CUPS

- ⅓ cup semisweet chocolate chips
- 3 tablespoons creamy peanut butter
- 1 tablespoon butter
- 4 cups plain popped popcorn
- ½ cup powdered sugar

1. Line baking sheet with waxed paper. Microwave chocolate chips, peanut butter and butter in medium microwavable bowl on HIGH 30 seconds; stir. Microwave 30 seconds or until melted and smooth. Pour mixture over popcorn in large bowl, stirring until evenly coated. Transfer to large resealable food storage bag.
2. Add powdered sugar to bag; seal bag. Shake until well coated. Spread on prepared baking sheets; cool completely. Store leftovers in airtight container in refrigerator.

POPCORN TRUFFLES

MAKES 40 TRUFFLES

- 8 cups popped plain popcorn
- 1 package (12 ounces) semisweet chocolate chips
- Colored sprinkles (optional)

1. Line two baking sheets with waxed paper. Place popcorn in large bowl.
2. Place chocolate chips in microwavable bowl. Microwave on HIGH 30 seconds; stir. Continue heating and stirring at 30-second intervals until melted and smooth. Pour over popcorn; stir until well coated.
3. Scoop popcorn mixture with small ice cream scoop, pressing mixture slightly against the inside of bowl; place on prepared baking sheets. Decorate with sprinkles, if desired. Let set at room temperature. Store in airtight container up to 3 days.

PARTY POPCORN

MAKES 12 CUPS

- ¼ cup vegetable oil
- ½ cup unpopped popcorn kernels
- 1 teaspoon fine sea salt or popcorn salt
- 4 ounces white almond bark,* chopped
- Rainbow nonpareils

***Look for almond bark by the chocolate chips in the baking aisle of the grocery store.**

1 Line two baking sheets with parchment paper.

2 Heat oil in large saucepan over medium-high heat. Add three popcorn kernels; cover and shake until kernels pop. Add remaining kernels; cover and cook until all kernels have popped, shaking saucepan frequently.

3 Spread popcorn on prepared baking sheets; immediately sprinkle with salt and toss gently to blend.

4 Melt almond bark according to package directions. Drizzle over popcorn; sprinkle with nonpareils. Let stand until set.

CRANBERRY CHOCOLATE CHIP CEREAL SQUARES

MAKES 2 TO 3 DOZEN BARS

- **6½ cups corn or rice cereal squares, divided**
- **½ cup (1 stick) butter**
- **1 package (6 ounces) dried cranberries (about 1⅓ cups)**
- **1 package (about 10 ounces) mini marshmallows**
- **1 cup semisweet chocolate chips**

1 Line 13×9-inch baking pan with foil, leaving 2-inch overhang on two sides. Spray with nonstick cooking spray.

2 Coarsely crush 2 cups cereal in large bowl with back of spoon or hands.

3 Melt butter in large saucepan over low heat. Add marshmallows; stir constantly until marshmallows are melted and mixture is smooth. Remove from heat; stir in remaining 4½ cups whole cereal, crushed cereal mixture and cranberries until well blended. Stir in chocolate chips. Press mixture into prepared pan.

4 Cover and refrigerate 30 minutes or until firm. Remove from pan using foil; cut into squares.

CHILI CASHEWS

MAKES 2 CUPS

- **1 tablespoon vegetable oil**
- **2 teaspoons chili powder**
- **1 teaspoon ground cumin**
- **½ teaspoon sugar**
- **½ teaspoon red pepper flakes**
- **2 cups roasted salted whole cashews (about 9 ounces)**

1 Preheat oven to 350°F. Line baking sheet with foil; spray with nonstick cooking spray.

2 Combine oil, chili powder, cumin, sugar and red pepper flakes in medium bowl; stir until well blended. Add cashews, stirring to coat evenly. Spread in single layer on prepared baking sheet.

3 Bake 8 to 10 minutes or until golden, stirring once. Cool completely on baking sheet.

S'MORE TREATS

MAKES 16 SQUARES

- 2½ cups chocolate crisp rice cereal
- 6 honey graham crackers, broken into ¼-inch pieces
- 3 tablespoons butter
- 1 tablespoon packed brown sugar
- 3½ cups mini marshmallows, divided
- ½ cup semisweet or milk chocolate chips, melted

1 Spray 9-inch square baking pan with nonstick cooking spray. Combine cereal and graham cracker pieces in large bowl.

2 Combine butter and brown sugar in large microwavable bowl; microwave on HIGH 25 to 30 seconds or until butter is melted. Add 2½ cups marshmallows; microwave on HIGH 1½ to 2 minutes or until mixture is melted and smooth, stirring after 1 minute. Pour over mixture; stir to coat. Fold in remaining 1 cup marshmallows.

3 Press evenly into prepared pan using waxed paper; cool completely. Drizzle with chocolate. Cut into squares.

TIP

For a slightly thicker treat, use an 8-inch square baking pan.

SPICY ROASTED CHICKPEAS >

MAKES 2 CUPS

- **1 can (about 15 ounces) chickpeas, rinsed and drained**
- **3 tablespoons olive oil**
- **½ teaspoon salt**
- **½ teaspoon black pepper**
- **¾ to 1 tablespoon chili powder**
- **⅛ to ¼ teaspoon ground red pepper**

1 Preheat oven to 400°F.

2 Combine chickpeas, oil, salt and black pepper in 13×9-inch baking pan; spread in single layer.

3 Bake 15 minutes or until chickpeas begin to brown, shaking pan twice.

4 Sprinkle with chili powder and red pepper. Bake 5 minutes or until dark golden-red. Cool before serving.

ROCKY ROAD BUNDLES

MAKES 1 DOZEN TREATS

- **1 cup semisweet chocolate chips**
- **½ cup creamy peanut butter**
- **1 package (3 ounces) ramen noodles,* broken into bite-size pieces**
- **1 cup mini marshmallows**

Use any flavor; discard seasoning packet.

1 Line baking sheet with waxed paper. Combine chocolate chips and peanut butter in large microwavable bowl. Microwave on MEDIUM (50%) 1 minute; stir. Continue heating and stirring at 15-second intervals until melted smooth.

2 Add noodles and marshmallows; mix well. Drop by tablespoonfuls onto prepared baking sheet; refrigerate 1 hour or until firm.

CHOCOLATE PEANUT POPCORN

MAKES 14 CUPS

- ¼ cup vegetable oil
- ½ cup unpopped popcorn kernels
- 2 cups roasted salted peanuts
- 1 package (about 12 ounces) semisweet chocolate chips
- 1 cup light corn syrup
- ¼ cup (½ stick) butter
- ½ teaspoon salt

1. Preheat oven to 300°F. Line two baking sheets with parchment paper.
2. Heat oil in large saucepan over medium-high heat. Add three popcorn kernels; cover and shake until kernels pop. Add remaining kernels; cover and cook until all kernels have popped, shaking saucepan frequently. Divide popcorn between prepared baking sheets; add 1 cup peanuts to each baking sheet and combine with popcorn.
3. Combine chocolate chips, corn syrup, butter and salt in medium saucepan; cook over medium heat until mixture boils, stirring constantly. Pour half of chocolate mixture over popcorn and peanuts on each baking sheet; stir until well coated.
4. Bake 25 to 30 minutes or until top is shiny but not sticky, stirring every 5 minutes. Cool on baking sheets 5 minutes; remove to bowl or plate, breaking up chunks into smaller pieces. Store in airtight container.

CRACKER TOFFEE

MAKES 24 SERVINGS

- **72 rectangular butter-flavored crackers**
- **1 cup (2 sticks) butter**
- **1 cup packed brown sugar**
- **¼ teaspoon salt**
- **2½ cups semisweet chocolate chips**
- **2 cups chopped pecans**

1. Preheat oven to 375°F. Line large baking sheet with foil. Spray generously with nonstick cooking spray. Arrange crackers with edges touching in pan.
2. Combine butter, brown sugar and salt in medium saucepan. Heat over medium heat until butter melts, stirring frequently. Increase heat to high; boil 3 minutes without stirring. Pour mixture evenly over crackers; spread to cover.
3. Bake 5 minutes. Immediately sprinkle chocolate chips evenly over crackers; spread to cover. Sprinkle pecans over chocolate, pressing down. Cool to room temperature; refrigerate 2 hours. Break into chunks to serve.

VARIATION

Substitute peanut butter chips for chocolate chips and coarsely chopped lightly salted peanuts for chopped pecans.

CURRIED CHICKPEA CRUNCH

MAKES ABOUT 2 CUPS

- **1 can (about 15 ounces) chickpeas, rinsed, drained and patted dry**
- **1½ teaspoons vegetable oil, divided**
- **1 teaspoon mild curry powder**
- **¼ teaspoon salt**
- **1 package (3 ounces) ramen noodles***
- **1 teaspoon packed brown sugar**

****Use any flavor; discard seasoning packet.***

1. Preheat oven to 375°F. Line baking sheet with parchment paper.
2. Place chickpeas, 1 teaspoon oil, curry powder and salt in medium bowl; mix well. Spread in even layer on prepared baking sheet. Bake 20 minutes.
3. Meanwhile, crumble noodles in same bowl. Add remaining ½ teaspoon oil and brown sugar; stir until well coated. Add to baking sheet; toss with chickpeas and spread in even layer.
4. Bake 15 minutes or until noodles are toasted and lightly browned. Cool on baking sheet 20 minutes.

ROSEMARY NUT MIX >

MAKES 4 CUPS

- 2 tablespoons butter
- 2 cups pecan halves
- 1 cup macadamia nuts
- 1 cup walnuts
- 1 teaspoon dried rosemary
- ½ teaspoon salt
- ¼ teaspoon red pepper flakes

1 Preheat oven to 300°F.

2 Melt butter in large saucepan over low heat. Stir in pecans, macadamia nuts and walnuts. Add rosemary, salt and red pepper flakes; cook and stir about 1 minute. Spread mixture on ungreased baking sheet.

3 Bake 8 to 10 minutes or until nuts are fragrant and lightly browned, stirring occasionally. Cool completely on baking sheet on wire rack.

PAPRIKA ALMONDS

MAKES 1 CUP

- 1 cup whole blanched almonds
- 1 teaspoon olive oil
- ¼ teaspoon coarse salt
- ¼ teaspoon smoked or sweet paprika

1 Preheat oven to 375°F. Spread almonds in single layer in shallow baking pan.

2 Bake 8 to 10 minutes or until almonds are lightly browned. Transfer to bowl; cool 5 to 10 minutes. Stir in oil, salt and paprika until well coated.

TIP

For the best flavor, serve these almonds the day they are made.

FRIED FAVORITES

TOASTED RAVIOLI

MAKES 20 TO 24 RAVIOLI

- 1 cup all-purpose flour
- 2 eggs
- ¼ cup water
- 1 cup plain dry bread crumbs
- 1 teaspoon Italian seasoning
- ¾ teaspoon garlic powder
- ¼ teaspoon salt
- ½ cup grated Parmesan cheese
- 2 tablespoons minced fresh parsley
- Vegetable oil for frying
- 1 package (12 to 16 ounces) meat or cheese ravioli, thawed if frozen
- Pasta sauce, heated

1. Place flour in shallow bowl. Whisk eggs and water in another shallow bowl. Combine bread crumbs, Italian seasoning, garlic powder and salt in third shallow bowl. Combine cheese and parsley in large bowl; stir to blend.
2. Heat 2 inches of oil in large deep skillet over medium-high heat to 350°F; adjust heat to maintain temperature during cooking.
3. Coat ravioli with flour. Dip in egg mixture, letting excess drip back into bowl. Roll in bread crumb mixture to coat.
4. Cook ravioli in batches 1 minute or until golden brown, turning once. Remove from oil with slotted spoon; drain on paper towel-lined plate. Add to bowl with cheese mixture; toss to coat. Serve with warm pasta sauce.

CRISPY MUSHROOMS

MAKES 4 SERVINGS

- ½ cup mayonnaise
- 2 teaspoons minced garlic
- 1 teaspoon lemon juice
- ½ cup all-purpose flour
- ½ cup garlic and herb-flavored bread crumbs
- ½ cup grated Parmesan cheese
- ½ teaspoon paprika
- ½ teaspoon salt
- ¼ teaspoon black pepper
- 2 eggs
- 1 teaspoon water
- 1 package (8 ounces) whole mushrooms, stems trimmed
- Vegetable oil for frying

1. For garlic mayonnaise, combine mayonnaise, garlic and lemon juice in small bowl; mix well.
2. Combine flour, bread crumbs, Parmesan cheese, paprika, salt and pepper in shallow bowl. Whisk eggs and water in another shallow bowl.
3. Using a fork, dip mushrooms into egg mixture, allowing excess to drip back into bowl. Roll in bread crumb mixture to coat.
4. Heat 1 inch of oil in large deep skillet over medium-high heat to 350°F; adjust heat to maintain temperature during cooking.
5. Cook mushrooms in batches 1 minute or until golden brown, turning once. Remove from oil with slotted spoon; drain on paper towel-lined plate. Serve warm with garlic mayonnaise.

ZUCCHINI FRITTE

MAKES 4 SERVINGS

- Lemon Aioli (recipe follows)
- Vegetable oil for frying
- ¾ to 1 cup soda water
- ½ cup all-purpose flour
- ¼ cup cornstarch
- ½ teaspoon salt
- ¼ teaspoon garlic powder
- ¼ teaspoon dried oregano
- ¼ teaspoon black pepper
- 3 cups panko bread crumbs
- 1½ pounds medium zucchini (6 to 8 inches long), ends trimmed, cut lengthwise into ¼-inch-thick slices
- ¼ cup grated Parmesan or Romano cheese
- Chopped fresh parsley

1. Prepare Lemon Aioli; cover and refrigerate until ready to use.
2. Line baking sheet with paper towels; set aside. Heat 2 inches of oil in large saucepan or Dutch oven over medium-high heat to 350°F; adjust heat to maintain temperature during cooking.
3. Meanwhile, pour ¾ cup soda water into large bowl. Whisk flour, cornstarch, salt, garlic powder, oregano and pepper in small bowl. Slowly whisk flour mixture into soda water just until blended. Add additional soda water if necessary to reach consistency of thin pancake batter. Place panko in medium bowl.
4. Working with one at a time, dip zucchini slices into batter to coat, letting excess batter drip back into bowl. Add to panko mixture; coat completely, pressing to adhere. Place zucchini on prepared baking sheet.
5. Cook zucchini in batches 3 to 4 minutes or until golden brown. Drain on paper towel-lined plate. Sprinkle with cheese and parsley; serve with Lemon Aioli.

LEMON AIOLI

Combine ½ cup mayonnaise, 2 tablespoons lemon juice, 1 tablespoon chopped fresh parsley and 1 teaspoon minced garlic in small bowl; mix well. Season with salt and pepper.

FRIED MACARONI AND CHEESE BITES

MAKES 48 PIECES

- 8 ounces uncooked elbow macaroni
- 2 tablespoons butter
- 2 tablespoons all-purpose flour
- 2 cups milk
- 1 teaspoon salt, divided
- 2 cups (8 ounces) shredded Cheddar cheese
- 1 cup (4 ounces) shredded Swiss cheese
- 1 cup (4 ounces) shredded smoked Gouda cheese
- Vegetable oil for frying
- 3 eggs
- ¼ cup water
- 2 cups plain dry bread crumbs
- 1 teaspoon Italian seasoning
- Marinara sauce, heated

1. Cook macaroni in large saucepan of boiling salted water 7 minutes or until al dente. Drain and set aside.
2. Melt butter in medium saucepan over medium-high heat. Whisk in flour until smooth. Cook 1 minute, whisking frequently. Whisk in milk in thin, steady stream; cook over medium heat 8 minutes or until thickened. Add ½ teaspoon salt. Gradually stir in cheeses until melted and smooth. Stir in macaroni.
3. Spray 9-inch square baking pan with nonstick cooking spray. Spread macaroni and cheese in prepared pan; smooth top. Cover with plastic wrap; refrigerate 4 hours or until firm and cold.
4. Turn out macaroni and cheese onto cutting board; cut into 48 pieces. Heat ½ inch oil in large deep skillet or saucepan over medium-high heat to 350°F; adjust heat to maintain temperature during cooking.
5. Beat eggs and ¼ cup water in shallow dish. Combine bread crumbs, Italian seasoning and remaining ½ teaspoon salt in another shallow dish. Working with a few pieces at a time, dip macaroni and cheese pieces in egg, then roll in bread crumb mixture to coat. Place on large baking sheet. Dip coated pieces in egg mixture again; roll in bread crumb mixture to coat.
6. Cook in batches 3 minutes or until golden brown, turning once. Drain on paper towel-lined wire rack. Serve warm with marinara sauce for dipping.

FRIED CAULIFLOWER WITH GARLIC TAHINI SAUCE

MAKES 8 SERVINGS

SAUCE

- ½ cup tahini
- ¼ cup plain Greek yogurt
- 2 tablespoons lemon juice
- 2 cloves garlic, minced
- ¼ teaspoon salt
- 6 tablespoons water
- 1 tablespoon minced fresh parsley

CAULIFLOWER

- 1 cup all-purpose flour
- 1½ teaspoons salt, divided
- Black pepper
- 4 eggs
- ¼ cup water
- 2 cups panko bread crumbs
- 1 teaspoon ground cumin
- 1 teaspoon garlic powder
- ¼ teaspoon ground nutmeg
- 1 large head cauliflower (2½ pounds), cut into 1-inch florets
- Vegetable oil for frying

1. For sauce, whisk tahini, yogurt, lemon juice, garlic and ¼ teaspoon salt in medium bowl. Whisk in enough water in thin, steady stream until sauce is thinned to desired consistency. Stir in parsley.
2. For cauliflower, whisk flour, ½ teaspoon salt and pepper in large bowl. Whisk eggs and ¼ cup water in medium bowl. Combine panko, remaining 1 teaspoon salt, cumin, garlic powder and nutmeg in large bowl. Toss cauliflower florets in flour mixture to coat; tap off excess. Dip in egg mixture, letting excess drain back into bowl. Place in panko mixture; toss until coated. Place breaded cauliflower on baking sheet.
3. Heat 2 inches of oil in large saucepan over medium-high heat to 350°F; adjust heat to maintain temperature during cooking. Cook cauliflower in batches 4 minutes or until browned and tender, stirring once or twice. Drain on paper towel-lined baking sheet. Serve warm with sauce.

SPICY CRISPY SHRIMP

MAKES 4 SERVINGS

- ½ cup mayonnaise
- 4 teaspoons Thai chili sauce
- 1 teaspoon honey
- ½ teaspoon rice vinegar
- ¾ cup buttermilk
- 1 egg
- ¾ cup all-purpose flour
- ½ cup panko bread crumbs
- 1 teaspoon salt
- ½ teaspoon ground sage
- ½ teaspoon black pepper
- ¼ teaspoon onion powder
- ¼ teaspoon garlic powder
- ¼ teaspoon dried basil
- 16 to 20 large raw shrimp, peeled, deveined and patted dry
- Vegetable oil for frying
- 2 green onions, thinly sliced (optional)

1. For sauce, combine mayonnaise, chili sauce, honey and vinegar in small bowl; mix well. Cover and refrigerate until ready to serve.
2. Beat buttermilk and egg in shallow dish until well blended. Combine flour, panko, salt, sage, pepper, onion powder, garlic powder and basil in another shallow dish; mix well. Dip shrimp in buttermilk mixture, then in flour mixture, turning to coat completely. Place breaded shrimp on large plate; refrigerate until oil is hot.
3. Heat 2 inches of oil in large saucepan over medium-high heat to 350°F; adjust heat to maintain temperature during cooking. Cook shrimp in batches 2 to 3 minutes or until golden brown, turning once. Drain on paper towel-lined baking sheet.
4. Transfer shrimp to large bowl; add sauce and toss gently to coat. Garnish with green onions.

GREEN BEAN FRIES

MAKES 4 TO 6 SERVINGS

- 8 ounces fresh green beans, trimmed
- ½ cup all-purpose flour
- ½ cup cornstarch
- ¾ cup milk
- 1 egg
- 1 cup plain dry bread crumbs
- 1 teaspoon salt
- ½ teaspoon onion powder
- ¼ teaspoon garlic powder
- Vegetable oil for frying
- Ranch dressing for dipping

1. Bring large saucepan of salted water to a boil. Add green beans; cook 4 minutes or until crisp-tender. Drain and run under cold water to stop cooking.
2. Combine flour and cornstarch in large bowl. Beat milk and egg in another large bowl. Combine bread crumbs, salt, onion powder and garlic powder in shallow dish. Add beans to flour mixture; toss to coat. Working in batches, coat beans with egg mixture, letting excess drain back into bowl. Roll in bread crumb mixture to coat. Place on large baking sheet.
3. Heat 3 inches of oil in large saucepan over medium-high heat to 375°F; adjust heat to maintain temperature during cooking. Cook beans in batches 1 minute or until golden brown. Drain on paper towel-lined plate. Serve warm with ranch dressing.

SHRIMP RAMEN EGG ROLLS

MAKES 10 EGG ROLLS

- **1 tablespoon vegetable oil**
- **8 ounces small raw shrimp, peeled, deveined and coarsely chopped**
- **1 cup diced red bell pepper**
- **1 package (3 ounces) shrimp-flavored ramen noodles**
- **2 tablespoons chopped green onion**
- **10 egg roll wrappers**
- **Vegetable oil for frying**
- **Sweet and sour sauce**

1 Heat 1 tablespoon oil in large skillet over medium-high heat. Add shrimp and bell pepper; cook and stir 5 minutes or until shrimp are pink and opaque and bell pepper is softened. Transfer to large bowl.

2 Break noodles into large chunks; set seasoning packet aside. Cook noodles according to package directions; drain and rinse under cold water to stop cooking. Add noodles to bowl with shrimp. Stir in reserved seasoning packet and green onion; mix well.

3 Place one egg roll wrapper on work surface with one corner facing you. Place 2 tablespoons filling across center. Fold bottom and sides in over filling; roll up. Moisten edge with water to seal. Repeat with remaining wrappers and filling.

4 Heat 1 inch of oil in large deep skillet to 350°F; adjust heat to maintain temperature during cooking. Cook egg rolls in batches about 2 minutes per side or until golden brown. Drain on paper towels. Serve with sweet and sour sauce.

VARIATION

To bake egg rolls, preheat oven to 375°F. Brush tops of egg rolls with vegetable oil; bake 15 minutes or until crisp.

MOZZARELLA STICKS

MAKES 12 STICKS

- ¼ cup all-purpose flour
- 2 eggs
- 1 tablespoon water
- 1 cup plain dry bread crumbs
- 2 teaspoons Italian seasoning
- ½ teaspoon salt
- ½ teaspoon garlic powder
- 1 package (12 ounces) string cheese (12 sticks)
- Vegetable oil for frying
- 1 cup marinara or pizza sauce, heated

1. Place flour in shallow bowl. Whisk eggs and water in another shallow bowl. Combine bread crumbs, Italian seasoning, salt and garlic powder in third shallow bowl. Place large wire rack over paper towels.
2. Coat each piece of cheese with flour. Dip in egg mixture, letting excess drip back into bowl. Roll in bread crumb mixture to coat. Dip again in egg mixture and roll again in bread crumb mixture. Place on plate; refrigerate until ready to cook.
3. Heat 2 inches of oil in large saucepan over medium-high heat to 350°F; adjust heat to maintain temperature during cooking. Add cheese sticks; cook 1 minute or until golden brown. Drain on prepared wire rack. Serve with warm marinara sauce.

ZESTY LEMON-PEPPER WINGS

MAKES 8 SERVINGS

- 2 pounds chicken wings, tips discarded, separated at joints
- ⅔ cup all-purpose flour
- 1 teaspoon garlic powder
- 1 teaspoon onion powder
- ¾ teaspoon salt
- ½ teaspoon paprika
- ½ teaspoon black pepper
- Vegetable oil for frying
- ¼ cup (½ stick) butter, melted
- 2 tablespoons lemon-pepper seasoning
- 1 teaspoon dried parsley flakes
- Ranch dressing for dipping
- Lemon wedges and vegetable sticks (optional)

1 Place wings in large resealable food storage bag. Combine flour, garlic powder, onion powder, salt, paprika and pepper in small bowl; mix well. Add to bag with chicken; seal bag and toss to coat.

2 Heat 3 inches of oil in large saucepan over medium-high heat to 350°F; adjust heat to maintain temperature during cooking. Set wire rack over paper towels.

3 Add wings to hot oil; cook 10 minutes or until crisp and browned and chicken is cooked through, stirring occasionally. Drain on prepared wire rack.

4 Combine butter, lemon-pepper and parsley flakes in large bowl; mix well. Add wings; toss well to coat. Serve immediately with ranch dressing, lemon wedges and vegetables, if desired.

EXOTIC VEGGIE CHIPS

MAKES ABOUT 6 SERVINGS

- 3 tropical tubers (malanga, yautia, lila and/or taro roots)*
- 1 to 2 green (unripe) plantains
- 2 parsnips, peeled
- 1 medium sweet potato, peeled
- 1 lotus root*
- Vegetable oil for frying
- Coarse salt

*These tropical tubers are all similar and their labels are frequently interchangeable or overlapping. They are available in the produce section of Latin markets. Choose whichever tubers are available and fresh. Look for firm roots without signs of mildew or soft spots.

1. Line baking sheets with paper towels.
2. Peel thick shaggy skin from tubers; rinse tubers and pat dry. Thinly slice tubers with mandoline or sharp knife; place in single layer on prepared baking sheets to absorb excess moisture. (Stack in multiple layers with paper towels between layers.) Peel plantain; slice and place on paper towels. Slice parsnips and sweet potato and place on paper towels. Trim lotus root and remove tough skin with paring knife. Slice and place on paper towels.
3. Heat 3 inches of oil in large saucepan over medium-high heat to 350°F; adjust heat to maintain temperature during cooking. Working in batches, fry each vegetable until crisp and slightly curled, stirring occasionally. (Frying time will vary from 2 to 6 minutes depending on the vegetable.)
4. Remove vegetables with slotted spoon and drain on paper towels; immediately sprinkle with salt. Cool completely. Store in airtight containers at room temperature.

CHURROS

MAKES ABOUT 3 DOZEN CHURROS

- 1 cup water
- ¼ cup (½ stick) butter
- 6 tablespoons sugar, divided
- ¼ teaspoon salt
- 1 cup all-purpose flour
- 2 eggs
- Hot Fudge Sauce (page 157)
- Vegetable oil for frying
- 1 teaspoon ground cinnamon

1. Place water, butter, 2 tablespoons sugar and salt in medium saucepan; bring to a boil over high heat. Remove from heat. Add flour; beat with spoon until dough forms a ball and releases from side of pan. Vigorously beat in eggs, one at a time, until mixture is smooth. Spoon dough into pastry bag fitted with large star tip. Pipe 3×1-inch strips onto waxed paper-lined baking sheet. Freeze 20 minutes.
2. Meanwhile, prepare Hot Fudge Sauce.
3. Heat 1 inch of oil in large deep skillet to 375°F; adjust heat to maintain temperature during cooking. Loosen churros from baking sheet with large spatula. Cook churros in batches 3 to 4 minutes or until golden brown, turning once. Remove with slotted spoon; drain on paper towels.
4. Combine remaining 4 tablespoons sugar and cinnamon in paper bag. Add warm churros, one at a time. Close bag and shake until churros are coated with cinnamon-sugar mixture. Remove to wire rack; serve warm with Hot Fudge Sauce. Store tightly covered at room temperature or freeze up to 3 months.

HOT FUDGE SAUCE

MAKES ABOUT 2 CUPS

- 1 cup whipping cream
- ¼ cup light corn syrup
- 6 tablespoons packed dark brown sugar
- 4 ounces bittersweet chocolate, chopped
- 3 tablespoons unsweetened cocoa powder
- ½ teaspoon salt
- 2 tablespoons cold butter

1 Combine cream, corn syrup and brown sugar in large saucepan. Bring to a boil over medium-high heat; cook 2 minutes, stirring occasionally. Reduce heat to low. Whisk in chocolate, cocoa and salt; cook and stir 1 minute or until chocolate is melted and mixture is smooth. Remove from heat; whisk in butter.

2 Cool slightly; serve warm. Store leftovers in airtight container in refrigerator up to 2 weeks; reheat before serving.

DIPS & SPREADS

CRAB SHACK DIP

MAKES ABOUT 3½ CUPS

- ½ (8-ounce) package cream cheese, softened
- ½ cup sour cream
- 2 tablespoons mayonnaise
- ¾ teaspoon seasoned salt
- ¼ teaspoon paprika, plus additional for garnish
- 2 cans (6 ounces each) crabmeat, drained and flaked
- ½ cup (2 ounces) shredded mozzarella cheese
- 2 tablespoons minced onion
- 2 tablespoons finely chopped green bell pepper or jalapeño pepper
- Chopped fresh parsley (optional)
- Tortilla chips

1. Preheat oven to 350°F.
2. Combine cream cheese, sour cream, mayonnaise, seasoned salt and ¼ teaspoon paprika in medium bowl; stir until smooth and well blended. Add crabmeat, mozzarella, onion and bell pepper; stir until blended. Spread in small (1-quart) shallow baking dish.
3. Bake 15 to 20 minutes or until dip is bubbly and top is beginning to brown. Garnish with parsley and additional paprika; serve with tortilla chips.

CORN SALSA

MAKES ABOUT 2½ CUPS

- 1 large poblano pepper
- 1 package (16 ounces) frozen white or yellow corn
- ¼ cup diced red onion
- ¼ cup chopped fresh cilantro
- 1 large jalapeño pepper, seeded and finely chopped
- 1 tablespoon lime juice
- 1 tablespoon lemon juice
- ½ teaspoon salt
- ⅛ teaspoon black pepper

1. Preheat oven to 400°F. Line small baking pan with foil.
2. Roast poblano pepper on prepared pan about 40 minutes or until skin is charred and blistered, turning occasionally. Remove pepper to small bowl; cover with plastic wrap and let stand 10 minutes to loosen skin. Peel and dice pepper, discarding stem and seeds.
3. Meanwhile, cook corn according to package directions. Place in large bowl; refrigerate or freeze until cool.
4. Add poblano, onion, cilantro, jalapeño, lime juice, lemon juice, salt and pepper to corn; mix well. Let stand at least 30 minutes to blend flavors.

JALAPEÑO FETA DIP

MAKES ABOUT 1 CUP

- 1 jalapeño pepper, halved, stemmed and seeded
- ½ red onion, halved and separated
- 3 tablespoons plus 1 teaspoon olive oil, divided
- 8 ounces feta cheese
- 1 tablespoon water

1. Preheat oven to 400°F. Place jalapeño and onion on small baking sheet; drizzle with 1 teaspoon oil and stir to coat. Arrange vegetables cut sides down on baking sheet. Bake 20 minutes or until vegetables are softened and slightly charred around edges. Let stand until cool enough to handle.
2. Scrape skin from jalapeño with paring knife. Coarsely chop jalapeño and onion.
3. Combine feta, remaining 3 tablespoons oil and water in food processor; process until smooth and fluffy. Add vegetables; pulse 6 to 8 times or until blended but still chunky. Store dip in airtight container in refrigerator up to 1 week.

TIP

Serve this dip with a sliced baguette, pita bread wedges, pita chips and/or cut-up fresh vegetables. Or you can use it as a spread on toast, sandwiches and wraps.

WHITE SPINACH QUESO

MAKES 4 TO 6 SERVINGS

- 1 tablespoon olive oil
- 1 clove garlic, minced
- 1 tablespoon all-purpose flour
- 1 can (12 ounces) evaporated milk
- ½ teaspoon salt
- 2 cups (8 ounces) shredded Monterey Jack cheese, divided
- 1 package (10 ounces) frozen chopped spinach, thawed and squeezed dry
- Optional toppings: pico de gallo, guacamole, chopped fresh cilantro and queso fresco
- Tortilla chips

1 Preheat broiler.

2 Heat oil in medium saucepan over medium-low heat. Add garlic; cook and stir 1 minute without browning. Add flour; whisk until smooth. Add evaporated milk in thin, steady stream, whisking constantly. Stir in salt. Cook about 4 minutes or until slightly thickened, whisking frequently. Add 1½ cups Monterey Jack; whisk until smooth. Stir in spinach. Pour into medium cast iron skillet; sprinkle with remaining ½ cup Monterey Jack.

3 Broil 1 minute or until cheese is melted and browned in spots. Top with pico de gallo, guacamole, cilantro and queso fresco. Serve immediately with tortilla chips.

TIROKAFTERI (SPICY GREEK FETA SPREAD)

MAKES 2 CUPS

- 2 small hot red peppers
- ½ small clove garlic
- 1 block (8 ounces) feta cheese
- ¾ cup plain Greek yogurt
- 1 tablespoon lemon juice
- ½ teaspoon salt
- Toasted sliced French bread and/or cut-up fresh vegetables

1. Preheat oven to 400°F. Line small baking sheet with foil; place peppers on prepared baking sheet.
2. Bake 15 minutes or until peppers are soft and charred. Cool completely. Scrape off skin with paring knife. Cut off top and remove seeds. Place peppers in food processor. Add garlic; pulse until finely chopped.
3. Add feta, yogurt, lemon juice and salt; pulse until well blended but still chunky. Serve with bread and vegetables. Store leftovers in airtight container in refrigerator up to 2 weeks.

SPINACH-ARTICHOKE DIP

MAKES 6 TO 8 SERVINGS

- 1 package (8 ounces) baby spinach
- 1 package (8 ounces) cream cheese, softened
- ¼ cup mayonnaise
- 1 clove garlic, minced
- 1 teaspoon dried basil
- ½ teaspoon dried thyme
- ¼ teaspoon salt
- ¼ teaspoon red pepper flakes
- ¼ teaspoon black pepper
- 1 can (about 14 ounces) artichoke hearts, drained and chopped
- ¾ cup grated Parmesan cheese, divided
- Toasted French bread slices or tortilla chips

1. Preheat oven to 350°F. Spray 8-inch oval, round or square baking dish with nonstick cooking spray.
2. Place spinach in large microwavable bowl; cover and microwave on HIGH 2 minutes or until wilted. Uncover; let stand until cool enough to handle. Squeeze dry and coarsely chop.
3. Beat cream cheese, mayonnaise, garlic, basil, thyme, salt, red pepper flakes and black pepper in medium bowl until well blended. Stir in spinach, artichokes and ½ cup Parmesan. Spread in prepared baking dish; sprinkle with remaining ¼ cup Parmesan.
4. Bake about 30 minutes or until edges are golden brown. Cool slightly; serve warm with toasted bread slices.

BUFFALO CHICKEN DIP

MAKES 5 CUPS

- 2 packages (8 ounces each) cream cheese, softened and cut into pieces
- 1 jar (12 ounces) restaurant-style wing sauce
- 1 cup ranch dressing
- 2 cups shredded cooked chicken (from 1 pound boneless skinless chicken breasts)
- 2 cups (8 ounces) shredded Cheddar cheese
- Tortilla chips
- Celery sticks

1. Combine cream cheese, wing sauce and ranch dressing in large saucepan; cook over medium-low heat 7 to 10 minutes or until cream cheese is melted and mixture is smooth, whisking frequently.
2. Combine chicken and Cheddar cheese in large bowl. Add cream cheese mixture; stir until well blended. Pour into serving bowl; serve warm with tortilla chips and celery sticks.

CLASSIC GUACAMOLE

MAKES ABOUT 2 CUPS

- 4 tablespoons finely chopped white onion, divided
- 1 to 2 serrano or jalapeño peppers, seeded and finely chopped
- 1½ tablespoons coarsely chopped fresh cilantro, divided
- ¼ teaspoon minced garlic
- 2 large ripe avocados
- 1 medium tomato, peeled and chopped
- 1 to 2 teaspoons lime juice
- ¼ teaspoon salt
- Tortilla chips

1 Combine 2 tablespoons onion, serrano pepper, 1 tablespoon cilantro and garlic in large mortar. Grind with pestle until almost smooth. (Mixture can be processed in food processor, if necessary, but will become watery.)

2 Scoop avocado into in large bowl. Add pepper mixture; mash roughly, leaving avocado slightly chunky. Stir in tomato, lime juice, salt, remaining 2 tablespoons onion and ½ tablespoon cilantro; mix well. Serve with tortilla chips.

TZATZIKI DIP

MAKES ABOUT 3 CUPS

- 1 cup finely diced peeled seedless cucumber
- 2 cups plain Greek yogurt
- Grated peel of 1 lemon
- 3 tablespoons lemon juice
- 2½ tablespoons minced fresh mint
- 2 tablespoons extra virgin olive oil
- 1 tablespoon minced garlic
- 2 teaspoons salt
- 1½ teaspoons white wine vinegar
- Grape tomatoes and cut up carrots, bell peppers and/or zucchini

1. Wrap cucumber in paper towels or clean dish towel. Twist towel to squeeze juice from cucumber.
2. Combine cucumber, yogurt, lemon peel, lemon juice, mint, oil, garlic, salt and vinegar in medium bowl; mix well. Transfer to serving bowl; cover and refrigerate at least 2 hours.
3. Serve dip with vegetables.

WARM PEANUT-CARAMEL DIP >

MAKES 1¾ CUPS

- 1 jar (16 ounces) caramel ice cream topping
- ¾ cup creamy peanut butter
- ½ cup milk
- Apple slices and pretzel twists

1. Combine caramel topping, peanut butter and milk in small saucepan. Heat over low heat until mixture is melted and smooth, stirring constantly.
2. Pour into serving bowl. Serve with apple slices and pretzels.

SALSA FRESCA

MAKES 2 CUPS

- 1½ cups finely chopped tomatoes
- ¼ cup finely chopped red onion
- 1 to 2 serrano or jalapeño peppers, stemmed, seeded and minced*
- 2 tablespoons finely chopped fresh cilantro
- 1 teaspoon lime juice
- ½ teaspoon salt
- Tortilla chips

***Add one pepper to salsa; taste and add additional pepper for spicier salsa.**

1. Combine tomatoes, onion, 1 serrano pepper, cilantro, lime juice and salt in medium bowl. Taste and add additional pepper for spicier salsa.
2. Let stand 30 minutes to 1 hour to allow flavors to blend.

HOT CHEESE-CHIPOTLE DIP

MAKES 8 SERVINGS (3 CUPS)

- 2 tablespoons butter
- 1 onion, chopped
- ½ red bell pepper, finely chopped
- 1 clove garlic, minced
- 2 tablespoons all-purpose flour
- 1 can (about 14 ounces) diced tomatoes, drained and 2 tablespoons juice reserved
- 1 cup lager or pilsner beer, preferably Mexican
- 1 canned chipotle pepper in adobo sauce, minced, plus 1 teaspoon adobo sauce
- 4 cups (16 ounces) shredded Mexican-style cheese blend
- Chopped fresh cilantro (optional)
- Tortilla chips

1. Melt butter in medium saucepan over medium heat. Add onion, bell pepper and garlic; cook and stir 5 minutes or until tender. Add flour; stir until well blended. Stir in tomatoes and reserved juice, lager, chipotle pepper and adobo sauce; bring to a boil. Reduce heat to low; simmer 5 minutes or until thickened.
2. Remove from heat. Add cheese blend, 1 cup at a time, stirring until melted after each addition. If necessary, return to very low heat and stir just until melted (do not overcook or the cheese will become gritty).
3. Transfer to serving bowl. Sprinkle with cilantro, if desired. Serve warm with tortilla chips.

VEGETABLE-TOPPED HUMMUS

MAKES ABOUT 1 CUP

- 1 can (about 15 ounces) chickpeas, rinsed and drained
- ½ cup tahini
- 2 tablespoons lemon juice
- 1 clove garlic
- ¾ teaspoon salt
- 1 tomato, finely chopped
- 2 green onions, finely chopped
- 2 tablespoons minced fresh parsley
- Pita bread rounds or assorted crackers (optional)

1. Combine chickpeas, tahini, lemon juice, garlic and salt in food processor or blender; process until smooth.
2. Combine tomato, green onions and parsley in small bowl; mix well.
3. Spoon hummus into serving bowl; top with tomato mixture. Serve with pita bread rounds or assorted crackers, if desired.

CREAMY VEGETABLE DIP

MAKES 2 CUPS

- 2 packages (8 ounces each) cream cheese, softened
- ½ cup finely chopped broccoli
- ½ cup shredded carrot
- 2 tablespoons milk
- 2 tablespoons sliced green onion
- 1 tablespoon lemon juice
- 1 teaspoon grated lemon peel
- ½ teaspoon salt
- ½ teaspoon black pepper
- Assorted crackers

1 Beat cream cheese in medium bowl with electric mixer on medium speed until smooth. Add broccoli, carrot, milk, green onion, lemon juice, lemon peel, salt and pepper; mix until well blended.

2 Transfer to serving bowl. Cover and refrigerate until ready to serve. Serve with crackers.

GINGER-LEMON CHEESE SPREAD WITH PINEAPPLE-PEACH SAUCE

MAKES 8 SERVINGS

- 2 packages (8 ounces each) cream cheese, softened
- 1 cup sour cream
- 3 tablespoons packed brown sugar
- 1 tablespoon grated lemon peel
- ¾ teaspoon ground ginger
- ½ cup crushed pineapple, well drained
- ½ cup peach or apricot preserves
- Assorted crackers and sliced fresh fruit, such as apples and pears

1. Line 3-cup decorative mold or bowl with plastic wrap.
2. Beat cream cheese and sour cream in large bowl with electric mixer at medium speed just until creamy. Add brown sugar, lemon peel and ginger; beat until well blended.
3. Spoon cheese mixture into prepared mold. Cover with plastic wrap; refrigerate at least 8 hours or up to 2 days.
4. Just before serving, combine pineapple and peach preserves in small bowl. Unmold cheese spread onto serving plate. Spoon sauce around cheese. Serve with crackers and fruit.

CLASSIC CHEESE BALL

MAKES ABOUT 2½ CUPS

- 2 packages (8 ounces each) cream cheese, softened
- ⅓ cup mayonnaise
- ¼ cup grated Parmesan cheese
- 2 tablespoons finely chopped carrot
- 1 tablespoon finely chopped red onion
- 1½ teaspoons prepared horseradish
- ¼ teaspoon salt
- ½ cup chopped pecans or walnuts
- Crackers and bread sticks

1. Beat cream cheese in large bowl with electric mixer at medium speed until creamy. Add mayonnaise, Parmesan cheese, carrot, onion, horseradish and salt; beat until well blended. Cover and refrigerate until firm.
2. Shape cheese mixture into ball; roll in pecans. Wrap cheese ball in plastic wrap and refrigerate at least 1 hour. Serve with crackers and bread sticks.

METRIC CONVERSION CHART

VOLUME MEASUREMENTS (dry)

1/8 teaspoon = 0.5 mL
1/4 teaspoon = 1 mL
1/2 teaspoon = 2 mL
3/4 teaspoon = 4 mL
1 teaspoon = 5 mL
1 tablespoon = 15 mL
2 tablespoons = 30 mL
1/4 cup = 60 mL
1/3 cup = 75 mL
1/2 cup = 125 mL
2/3 cup = 150 mL
3/4 cup = 175 mL
1 cup = 250 mL
2 cups = 1 pint = 500 mL
3 cups = 750 mL
4 cups = 1 quart = 1 L

VOLUME MEASUREMENTS (fluid)

1 fluid ounce (2 tablespoons) = 30 mL
4 fluid ounces (1/2 cup) = 125 mL
8 fluid ounces (1 cup) = 250 mL
12 fluid ounces (1 1/2 cups) = 375 mL
16 fluid ounces (2 cups) = 500 mL

WEIGHTS (mass)

1/2 ounce = 15 g
1 ounce = 30 g
3 ounces = 90 g
4 ounces = 120 g
8 ounces = 225 g
10 ounces = 285 g
12 ounces = 360 g
16 ounces = 1 pound = 450 g

DIMENSIONS

1/16 inch = 2 mm
1/8 inch = 3 mm
1/4 inch = 6 mm
1/2 inch = 1.5 cm
3/4 inch = 2 cm
1 inch = 2.5 cm

OVEN TEMPERATURES

250°F = 120°C
275°F = 140°C
300°F = 150°C
325°F = 160°C
350°F = 180°C
375°F = 190°C
400°F = 200°C
425°F = 220°C
450°F = 230°C

BAKING PAN SIZES

Utensil	Size in Inches/Quarts	Metric Volume	Size in Centimeters
Baking or Cake Pan (square or rectangular)	8×8×2	2 L	20×20×5
	9×9×2	2.5 L	23×23×5
	12×8×2	3 L	30×20×5
	13×9×2	3.5 L	33×23×5
Loaf Pan	8×4×3	1.5 L	20×10×7
	9×5×3	2 L	23×13×7
Round Layer Cake Pan	8×1½	1.2 L	20×4
	9×1½	1.5 L	23×4
Pie Plate	8×1¼	750 mL	20×3
	9×1¼	1 L	23×3
Baking Dish or Casserole	1 quart	1 L	—
	1½ quart	1.5 L	—
	2 quart	2 L	—